yukibooks.com/b/633596

girl

Mädchen

boy

Junge

mommy

Mama

daddy

Papa

young
jung

old
alt

child

Kind

adult

Erwachsener

accept

akzeptieren

refuse

verweigern

yes

ja

no

nein

smile
lächeln

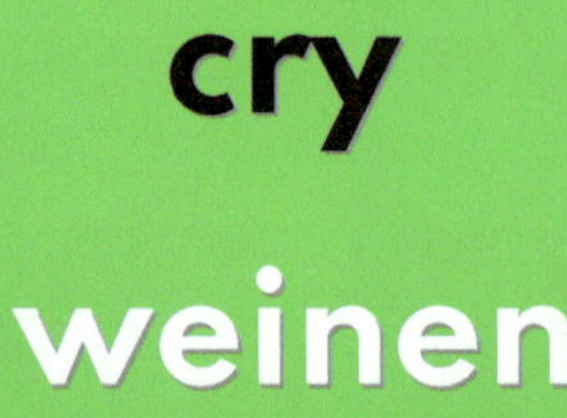

cry
weinen

happy

glücklich

sad

traurig

alone

allein

together

zusammen

noise

Lärm

quiet

ruhig

hot

heiß

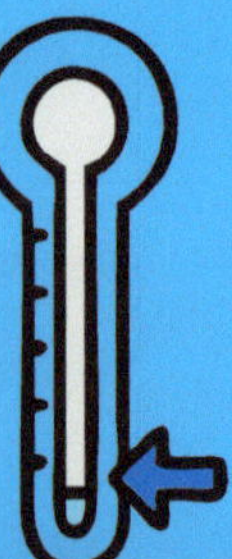

cold

kalt

a little

ein wenig

a lot

viel

solid

fest

liquid

flüssig

short

kurz

long

lang

slow

langsam

fast

schnell

tiny

winzig

small

klein

big

groß

huge

riesig

in

in

out

aus

inflated

aufgeblasen

deflated

entleert

on

auf

under

unter

dirty

dreckig

clean

sauber

identical

identisch

different

unterschiedlich

left

links

right

rechts

$$1 + 1 = 5$$

wrong

falsch

$$1 + 1 = 2$$

correct

korrekt

thin

dünn

thick

dick

easy

leicht

difficult

schwer

close

schließen

open

öffnen

tall
groß

short
klein

healthy

gesund

sick

krank

day

Tag

night

Nacht

play

spielen

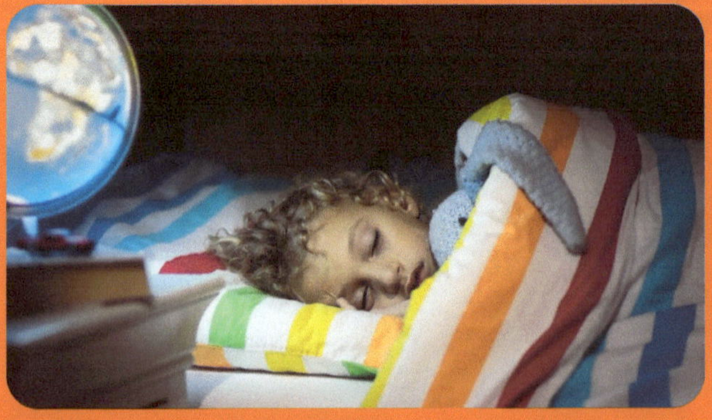

sleep

schlafen

sunny

sonnig

cloudy

wolkig

rainy

regnerisch

stormy

stürmisch

white

weiß

black

schwarz

light colors

helle Farben

dark colors

dunkle Farben

sweet
süß

sour
sauer

salty
salzig

bitter
bitter

whole

ganz

half

Hälfte

full

voll

empty

leer

eat

essen

drink

trinken

near

nah

far

fern

there

dort

here

hier

stand up

aufstehen

lay down

hinlegen

sit down

hinsetzen

curly hair
lockiges Haar
straight hair
glattes Haar

soaked

eingeweicht

wet

nass

dry

trocken

in front of

vor

behind

hinter

between

zwischen

beside

neben

roof

Dach

floor

Boden

heavy

schwer

light

licht

fragile

zerbrechlich

hardy

widerstandsfähig

weak

schwach

strong

stark

sharp

scharf

soft

weich

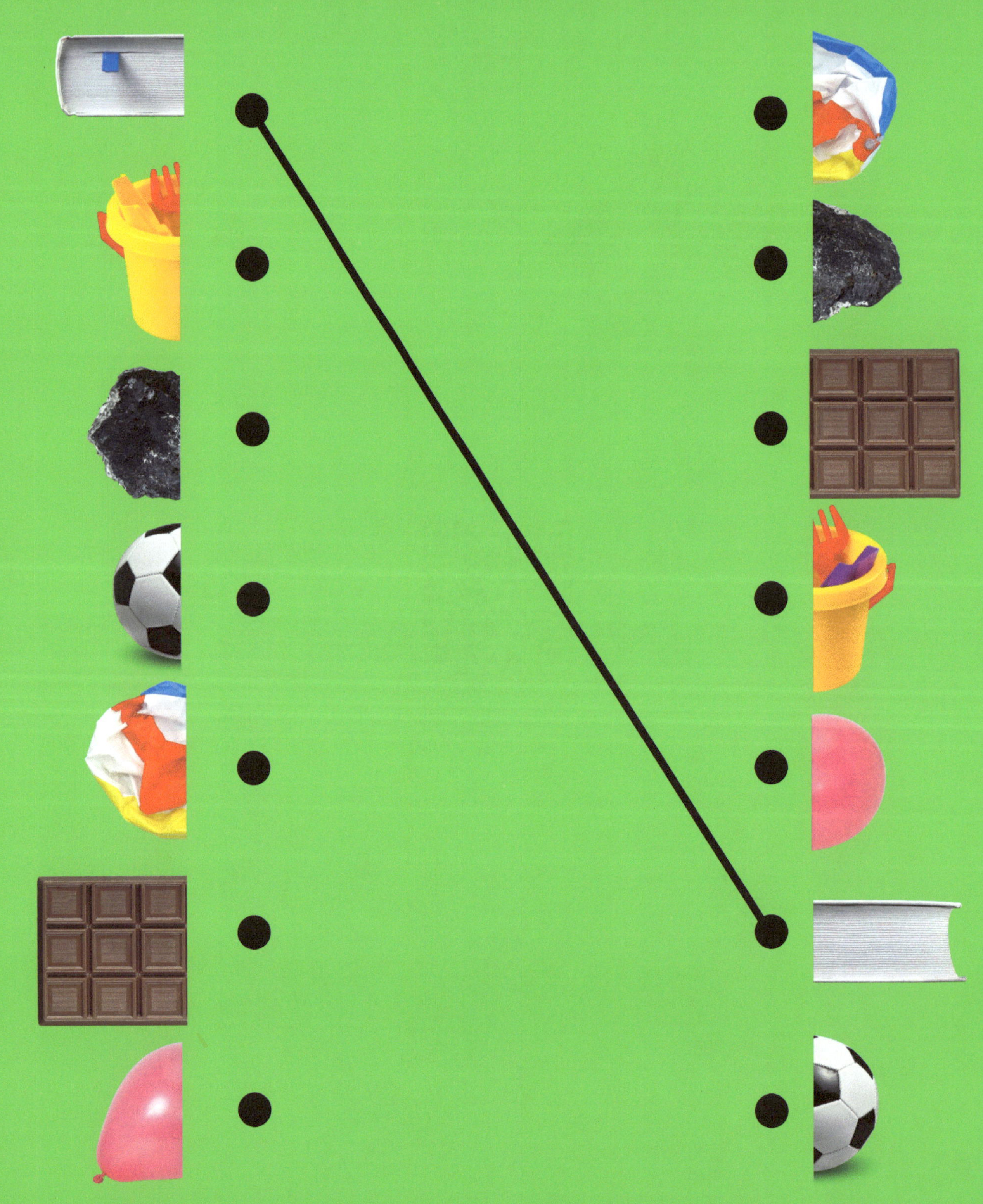